HANDIMALS

ANIMALS IN ART AND NATURE

SILVIA LOPEZ ART BY GUIDO DANIELE

Christy Ottaviano Books

HENRY HOLT AND COMPANY

NEW YORK

Guido Daniele

INTRODUCTION

Imagine a cave, thousands of years ago. A group of our ancestors huddle around a fire, tired after hunting for food. Their days are a constant struggle for survival. There is little time for much else. And yet, using the cave's surface as a canvas and whatever materials are available, these ancient artists are inspired to draw what their minds see. Today we still marvel at their stunning drawings of bison, deer, horses, boars, and mastodons.

For centuries, artists have painted animals on rock, papyrus, canvas, and wood. Images have been chiseled on stone, carved on gems, shaped from clay, and woven into cloth.

Artist Guido Daniele also loves the beauty, grace, and dignity he sees in animals. But he has chosen a very different canvas on which to place his art. He uses human hands, fingers, and arms. He calls his creations Handimals.

This book showcases sixteen examples of Guido's astonishing art. But like all art, they are only representations. Nature has already designed the individual features that make each animal perfect for its environment. Nature is the original artist.

Guido believes that the fate of the world's animals rests in human hands. His message is, "Hands should be used to create, not destroy." We hope that every Handimal will spark interest in the animal it represents and promote its survival. That's why the book also contains facts. The more we know about all the creatures that share our planet, the more we will understand the need to protect their rightful place on earth.

CHAMELEON

Grasping the branch with V-shaped feet, the chameleon rocks back and forth as it inches toward its next meal. Its swaying fools the insect into thinking the chameleon is a leaf waving in the breeze. Focused on its prey, the chameleon's eyes stare straight ahead. But the eyeballs can move independently. One pinpoint pupil may look up while the other whirls toward the ground. Swiveling eyes help the slow-walking reptile spot a meal, a mate, or a predator.

The chameleon's body may move slowly, but not its tongue. Often longer than its body, a chameleon's tongue zips out, sticks to the prey, and rolls back faster than human eyes can follow.

A relaxed chameleon's skin blends into its surroundings. But when it is afraid, wants to attract a mate, or needs to scare away a rival, the chameleon can alter the color and pattern of its skin in seconds. Even newborn chameleons can change their color.

TOUCAN

Short, doglike barks echoing through the jungles of Central and South America seem to say, "Here I am, the symbol of the rain forest!" But no dogs are in sight. The sounds are the calls of toucans.

The toucan's stocky body, bright round eyes, and strange toes (two facing front and two back) are already unique. But its really outstanding feature is its oversized beak, the biggest on any bird in proportion to body size. This remarkable beak is made of keratin, the same substance as human fingernails, and is surprisingly light. The muscles around it are weak, which do not allow the bird to bite down hard, but the beak is perfect for reaching fruit on the ends of branches too thin to hold the toucan's weight. It also serves to control body temperature: toucans do not sweat!

When they are ready for sleep, toucans twist their heads, rest their enormous beaks on their backs, and curl their tails forward. Slumbering toucans resemble balls topped by crowns of feathers.

GIANT PANDA

Deep in China's forest, a mother panda nurses a hairless pink cub not much bigger than a hot dog bun. Weighing about the same as a child's juice box, it is one of nature's smallest newborns compared to the adult it will become. Its eyes will not open for at least six weeks. Because cubs need care for over two years, female pandas have few babies in their lifetimes.

When giant pandas eat, they often sit much like humans: back legs stretched forward while front paws pull down bamboo, their main source of food. They have five fingers but use a specially shaped bone on the wrist as a thumb. Powerful jaw muscles—the reason for the panda's round face—are needed to grind tough stalks.

Giant pandas are classified as carnivores because their digestive systems are designed to eat meat. But they have adapted to habitats rich in bamboo plants and eat more than thirty pounds of it daily. Since it passes through the gut quickly, adult pandas go to the bathroom over forty times a day!

KOMODO DRAGON

In 1910, a Dutch soldier discovered giant lizards living on the island of Komodo, near Indonesia. The natives called them "oras" or "land crocodiles." The creatures moved with a side-to-side swish, their long, flickering tongues "smelling" the air for a possible meal. They seemed as fierce as dragons from the ancient myths.

Komodo dragons are the largest and heaviest of all lizards, reaching almost ten feet long and three hundred pounds. They hunt by hiding and waiting for prey to pass by, then moving at great speed and pouncing with sharp claws. A Komodo's teeth, as big as those of a large shark, are covered with a special skin that bleeds when the lizard bites, giving the impression that it has bloody saliva!

For years, scientists debated the Komodo's method of killing. Komodo saliva is packed with deadly bacteria. Scientists believed the giant lizards bit their victims and simply waited for them to die slowly of infection. But it was recently discovered that Komodos also have glands in their mouths that carry venom. It poisons smaller prey, which dies and is eaten quickly.

FLAMINGO

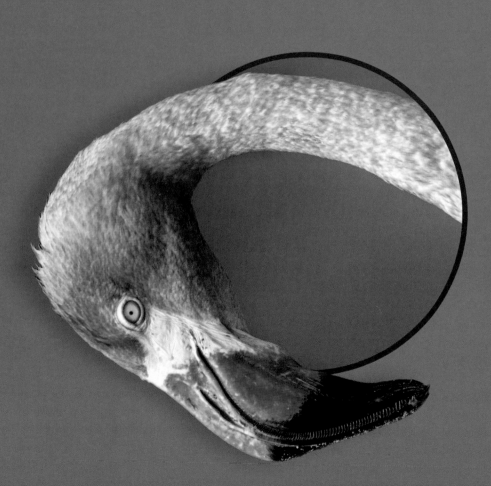

On webbed feet and legs like sticks, a flamingo wades into shallow water with the grace of a dancer. Its legs seem to bend backward at the knees, though those "knees" are really the bird's ankles! After stirring up the pond's bottom, the flamingo plunges its head underwater, flips it, and turns its curved bill into a scoop. Muddy water filters out along the sides. The small fish, crustaceans, and plants that remain become a flamingo meal.

Flamingos show their diet on the outside. A hatchling's feathers are white or pale gray. Later they will change color due to the shrimp and algae, rich in beta-carotene, that they consume. Feathers range from rosy pink to fiery orange-red depending on the species. But feather colors last only while the feathers are on the bird. Shed feathers return to being pale.

Newborn flamingos—whose bills are straight, not curved—are fed a liquid produced by both parents. Later, chicks will cluster in large groups. Though all look alike, adults will tell their own chicks apart by their calls.

AFRICAN ELEPHANT

Led by the matriarch—the oldest female—a herd of African elephants ambles toward a watering hole. A days-old calf is kept at the center of the herd, protected from predators. It already weighs almost three hundred pounds and drinks three gallons of its mother's milk a day!

The baby will grow to be the largest animal on land, bigger than its cousin the Asian elephant, with larger ears and a different body shape. But both species are among the smartest creatures in the world. They have excellent memories, form friendships, and grieve for dead companions.

An elephant's trunk is its most remarkable accessory. The trunk has thousands of muscles but no bones. It carries water and food to the elephant's mouth and can just as easily pull a heavy log as pick up a tiny straw. In the way humans use their hands, elephants use their trunk to greet, comfort, and caress one another.

ROYAL PYTHON

Sensing danger, a royal python curls into a tight ball, making it harder for predators—leopards, warthogs, large birds of prey—to turn it into a meal. This is the reason for the snake's other name: ball python.

So what is "royal" about the royal python? Not its size. It is the smallest of all African pythons, growing to about four feet. The name may come from a story about Queen Cleopatra of Egypt. It is said that she found the snake so beautiful that she wore it wrapped around her arm as jewelry.

When hungry, a royal python sticks out its tongue. If a potential meal—a rodent or bird—is nearby, the tongue senses a temperature change. Moving quickly, the snake bites and holds its prey. Like other constrictors, the royal python coils around the prey and squeezes the animal to death before swallowing it whole. A female royal python also curls around her clutch of eggs, but gently, to keep them warm. She goes without food until the babies hatch three months later!

MANDARIN DUCK

Guests at weddings in China may arrive bearing a gift of . . . ducks! Years ago, the birds could have been a live pair of mandarin ducks, though today they are probably made of wood or clay. In parts of Asia, mandarin ducks are thought to represent love and loyalty because the male and female stay together for life.

The male mandarin is considered one of the most beautiful ducks in the world. Its feathers are an explosion of colors and patterns. Not so for the female, whose feathers are unspectacular. But there is a good reason for that.

A female mandarin lays her eggs in tree hollows high off the ground. Her plain feathers blend with the shadows, disguising the nest from enemies like snakes, owls, and polecats. When babies are old enough, the mother jumps from the nest and signals for them to follow. They often tumble as far as twenty feet! If a predator approaches, mother mandarin may pretend she is hurt to lure the predator toward her and away from her ducklings.

MONARCH BUTTERFLY

It is early winter in central Mexico. Some forests seem covered in orange-and-black flowers. But a closer look shows these "flowers" are millions of monarch butterflies! They fly thousands of miles—on wingspans only inches long—from cold parts of North America to hibernate. When the season changes, they will set off for their northern home but make it only partway there. It takes four generations to complete the migration cycle.

In spring, the butterflies lift off the trees almost as one. They head back north, laying eggs on milkweed plants along the way and dying shortly after. Three more short-lived generations are born, each farther north, as in a relay race. Finally, the third generation arrives where their great-grandparents hatched. It lays the eggs for the fourth generation.

These fall monarchs have much longer life spans. As winter approaches, they begin the journey south. Once they reach the forest, they usually land—amazingly—on the *same tree* as their ancestors!

MORAY EEL

Unlike many fish, which cannot swim backward, a moray eel reverses its snakelike body into a crevice among the rocks. It keeps its head close to the lair's entrance, constantly gulping the current in order to breathe. The pattern on its scaleless skin helps it blend in.

The moray is waiting for dinner. It has poor eyesight but a great sense of smell. When its tubelike nostrils detect a passing fish, the eel lunges and clamps sharp, back-facing teeth onto its prey. Then something incredible happens. From deep inside the eel's throat, a *second set of jaws* thrusts forward. The jaws pull the fish back and down toward the eel's stomach! Moray eels are one of the few animals known in the world with these extending jaws.

A gaping mouth and sharp teeth make moray eels look fierce, but they are shy animals. They won't usually attack humans unless they feel threatened. Still, one bite can cause terrible wounds. A moray's jaws may lock, and the eel must then be pried off. To prevent attacks, some tourist areas discourage divers from hand-feeding moray eels.

ZEBRA

A herd of zebras—the correct name is a "dazzle"—makes its way across Africa's Serengeti Plain. It is taking part in the Great Migration, the largest land mammal migration on earth. Zebras are easy to spot. Their black-and-white stripes are actually different colors of fur—underneath the stripes, zebras are dark skinned!

Suddenly, the herd senses danger and breaks into a gallop, with the highest-ranking female in the lead. Stallions bring up the rear. A fast-running blur of stripes can confuse predators. If threatened, adult zebras also huddle around mothers with colts, their stripes blending in with the savanna's shadows and making individuals harder to pick out. Lions and hyenas know that a powerful kick from a hard, single-toed zebra hoof can cause serious injury.

Zebras also use their strong hooves for scraping dry streambeds. Water below the surface makes shallow drinking holes shared by many species. Zebras are social animals that sometimes create mixed herds with wildebeest and giraffes to warn one another of danger.

BALD EAGLE

A bald eagle glides, huge wings spread, thousands of feet above a sparkling lake. Even from that height, the bird can spot fish swimming far below. Oil droplets produced by the eagle's eyelids coat its eyes and cut the water's glare. The term "eagle eye" has never been truer.

Swooping down at great speed, the eagle skims the lake's surface, legs forward. Once over its prey, powerful toes tipped by razor-sharp nails, called talons, pluck the fish from the water and can kill it quickly by piercing the heart.

Bald eagles are not really bald. The name may come from the snowy feathers on their heads, or perhaps from the old English word "balde" meaning "white." These majestic animals have been America's symbol since 1782. The Great Seal of the United States features an eagle holding arrows and laurel leaves—symbols of war and peace—in its talons, legs wide open. It is the origin of the term "spread-eagle."

ALPACA

High in the Andes Mountains of South America, a herd of alpacas waits for shearing. Their fleece will be spun into wool, warmer and softer than a sheep's and as light as human hair. The alpacas do not mind. New coats will grow back in about a year.

Alpacas were prized in this area long before Columbus. Inca rulers counted them as part of their wealth, and alpaca-wool textiles were an important industry. But Conquistadors, seeking gold and silver, weren't interested in wool. They slaughtered alpacas to disrupt the Inca way of life. Native people, fleeing the Europeans, took some alpaca herds into the mountains. This may have saved the species.

The alpaca is good natured. It seems to wear a "smile" and hum when it is happy. But when it's upset—mostly at other alpacas but sometimes at humans—it spits! Alpaca spit is a green, grassy (and smelly) mix of saliva and half-digested food.

POLAR BEAR

At the top of the world, in a place known as the Arctic Ring of Life, a polar bear catches the scent of a seal swimming near an ice hole as far as a mile away. The bear approaches, then waits quietly. When the seal surfaces for air, the bear rushes to the hole, reaches in with a paw the size of a Frisbee, and, with luck, captures its next meal.

The seal provides blubber, essential to the polar bear's survival. Some meat may even be left behind and eaten by Arctic foxes or smaller bears. Protein is important, but for the magnificent predator classified as a sea mammal and called Nanuq by the native people, seal fat is life-giving.

During the summer months, when hunting is poor, the polar bear lives off its fat reserves. A four-inch layer of insulating blubber below the skin (which is black) helps keep the bear warm in any weather. So does a dense undercoat and the long tubelike hairs of its fur, which grows even on the pads of the feet. Polar bear fur is actually colorless! Air spaces in the hairs scatter the light, making the animal look white.

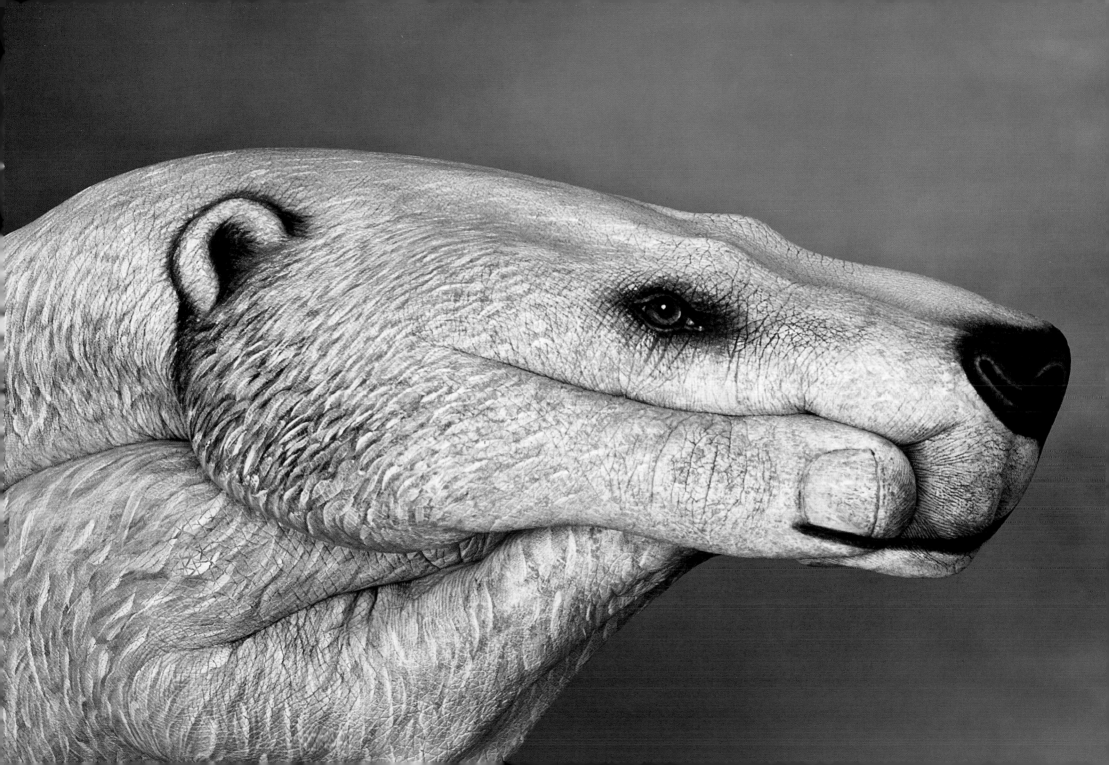

SEA TURTLE

Out in the ocean, a sea turtle swims steadily toward a beach. She has spent her life in the sea but must lay her eggs on land. Like her ancestors have done for millions of years, she travels for miles to return to the place where she hatched. She will lay her eggs in this same spot.

Under the cover of night, the turtle drags her heavy body—some species can weigh more than five hundred pounds—onto the sand. Choosing a place for a nest, she scoops out a hole with her back flippers and drops over one hundred eggs, round as Ping-Pong balls. Leathery shells keep the eggs from breaking. After covering the eggs with sand, the turtle heads for the water and, as silently as she came, swims back to the ocean.

Weeks later, baby turtles smaller than a child's hand scramble through the sand. They dash to the sea, toward the light of the horizon. Due to predators, few will make it to open water or adulthood. But those that survive will return to this beach to begin the ancient cycle once again.

DOLPHIN

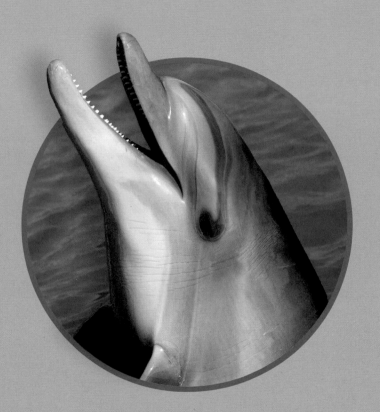

A pod of dolphins swims alongside a ship, leaping through its wake in playful sweeps. Tails snap. Jaws click. Dolphins communicate with body language. But they also make many sounds, though they lack vocal cords. The sounds, produced by an organ within their heads called a melon, bounce off objects and return as echoes to the dolphin's jaw. From there they travel to the inner ear. This process, known as echolocation, helps dolphins find food, as they lack a sense of smell. Study of dolphin communication has helped scientists develop underwater echolocation systems, such as sonar.

Like all sea mammals, a dolphin must breathe air. Mother dolphins nudge newborn calves to the surface for their first breaths. Others may do the same for an injured companion or even a struggling human swimmer. The dolphin is considered one of the most intelligent animals on earth.

MORE ABOUT THE...

CHAMELEON

★ Many of the approximately 160 chameleon species live on the island of Madagascar. Some are found in parts of Asia and southern Europe. No species inhabit North or South America.

★ Some tree-dwelling chameleons can hang upside down from their tails. But unlike many lizards, if the tail breaks off, it won't grow back.

★ Cutting down forests has caused several chameleons to become **endangered**. A few, like the fingertip-sized Brookesia bonsi, are **critically endangered** and may become extinct.

TOUCAN

★ The largest toucan, Toco toucan, is the one most people recognize. It appears in cartoons and on cereal boxes.

★ When a toucan is born, its beak is smaller in proportion to its size and grows as the bird gets older.

★ Most of the approximately forty species of toucans are spread over South America's rain forests. This has helped in their preservation. But some species are **vulnerable**. The Amazon's beautiful Ariel toucan is **endangered** due to loss of land.

GIANT PANDA

★ A little over one hundred years ago, only the red panda, a relative of raccoons, was called "panda." The giant panda was known as "black and white cat-footed animal."

★ Panda manure helps grow excellent tea plants.

★ Fewer than two thousand giant pandas, which the Chinese call "bear cat," live in the wild. In 1961, the panda was classified as **endangered** and became the symbol for the World Wildlife Fund. Better laws have helped pandas, but they are still **vulnerable**.

KOMODO DRAGON

★ Komodos have no predators—except each other. Larger dragons often eat smaller ones.

★ A Komodo will kill larger prey like water buffalo by rushing up and biting its legs. When the animal enters a pond to soak the wound, bacteria causes infection. The Komodo waits for the water buffalo to die . . . then eats it.

★ Komodos are a **vulnerable** species. Poachers set fires to scare out and catch deer and pigs, destroying Komodo food as well as habitat.

FLAMINGO

★ At rest, flamingos curl their necks backward and fold their heads mostly into their right wing. They tuck one leg under their bodies to help control body temperature.

★ Ancient Romans used flamingos as a food source. They especially loved flamingo tongues!

★ Flamingos exist in large numbers. Only the rare Andean flamingo from South America is considered **vulnerable**.

AFRICAN ELEPHANT

★ Ears help elephants control body temperature as blood circulates and cools beneath their thin skin. An African elephant's ears are shaped a little like the continent of Africa.

★ Prehistoric elephants were the size of large pigs. Today, the elephant's closest relative is a sea mammal: the manatee.

★ Loss of land, along with poaching—illegal trapping and killing—have caused African elephants to become a **vulnerable** species. Asian elephants are **endangered**.

ROYAL PYTHON

★ In parts of Central Africa, royal pythons are considered the symbol of the earth.

★ A giant prehistoric ancestor of constrictors like the royal python, called *Titanoboa*, was the size of a school bus, weighed 2,500 pounds, and ate crocodiles whole!

★ Royal pythons are not endangered, but their numbers are decreasing. The biggest threat comes from the pet trade, as whole clutches are taken from the wild to be sold.

MANDARIN DUCK

★ Mandarins make nests in hollows already lined with leaves, grass, or wood chips. When females leave the nest to eat, they pull out some of their own chest feathers and use them to keep the eggs warm.

★ Mandarins molt once a year. Males lose their colorful feathers, including their flight feathers. Since they can't fly at all during this time, they use camouflage to blend in.

★ There are few wild mandarin ducks in Asia due to loss of habitat. But some escaped from zoos and began small populations in other parts of the world.

MONARCH BUTTERFLY

★ Monarch populations are getting smaller since milkweed plants, the caterpillar's only food, are cleared to make way for farms or killed off by chemicals used on crops.

★ Milkweed is poisonous, but this does not affect the monarch. The butterfly stores the poison in its body for life. Its bright colors warn predators that the insect is toxic!

★ Some towns on the migration routes have started planting milkweed in gardens, parks, and ditches along roads to help the butterflies lay eggs.

MORAY EEL

★ Moray eels often make lairs from man-made objects like old pipes and shipwrecks.

★ Freshwater eels are eaten in many places, but morays do not make good food: their blood is poisonous and their flesh carries toxins that can cause illness.

★ A 1979 movie called *Alien* featured a monster from outer space that projected its teeth from its mouth. In 2007, scientists discovered the moray eel's second set of jaws. These jaws work a lot like those of the creature in the movie!

ZEBRA

★ Stripes extend all the way up through a zebra's mane. A padding of fat underneath keeps the short hair standing straight up.

★ Besides horses and donkeys, one other relative of the zebra is the rhinoceros!

★ All of Africa's zebras are losing land. Plains and mountain zebras are **near threatened** and **vulnerable**. Grévy's zebras (also known as imperial zebras) are **endangered**, with fewer than three thousand left in the wild.

BALD EAGLE

★ Bald eagles nearly died off in the 1940s due to a chemical called DDT, which was used as a pesticide. Once ingested, DDT harmed the eagles' reproductive cycle and caused thin eggshells that broke before eaglets could hatch. In the 1970s the United States banned DDT and passed the Endangered Species Act, helping the bald eagle make a comeback.

★ Bald eagle pairs build huge nests, sometimes eight feet across. Once eaglets can fly, adults will teach them how to hunt, fish, and steal prey from other birds.

★ There are eagle species all over the world. But bald eagles are found only in North America. Fossils of their ancestors date back one million years.

ALPACA

★ Alpacas and llamas look alike, but an alpaca's ears are straight and pointed while a llama's are curved like half-moons.

★ Like cattle and sheep, alpacas lack top front teeth. They bite off grass with hard gums and large lower teeth, then grind their food with their back teeth.

★ Alpacas in a herd all use the same spot—away from where they graze—to go to the bathroom. Having a huge pile of dung in one place keeps parasites from spreading.

POLAR BEAR

★ Every summer, hungry polar bears wander into the town of Churchill in Canada. Tourists on special expeditions take photos, which are often useful to researchers.

★ A female polar bear gives birth in the late fall inside a den she made in the snow. She lives off fat reserves, hibernating within the den until March, when she breaks through the ice and emerges with her cubs. Scientists call these babies COYs, which stands for cubs of the year.

★ Polar bears have no natural enemies, yet they are a **vulnerable** species. Human-influenced climate change is quickening the melting of Arctic ice.

SEA TURTLE

★ Climate change may affect sea turtles. The eggs do not start out as male or female; gender is determined by nest temperature. Warmer sand produces more females than males.

★ Unlike land turtles, sea turtles cannot pull their heads or flippers into their shells.

★ Less beach space has reduced nesting areas. Lights from buildings confuse hatchlings, which sometimes head inland. Out in the sea, the turtles often become "bycatch" and drown tangled in fishing nets. These factors have caused some sea turtles to become **vulnerable**. Green sea turtles are considered **endangered**. Hawksbill and Kemp's ridley turtles are **critically endangered**.

DOLPHIN

★ The world's oceans are home to most of the approximately forty species of dolphins. Others are found in certain rivers and seas. But none live in the icy waters near the North or South Poles.

★ One of the dolphin's closest living relatives is the hippopotamus.

★ The largest member of the dolphin family—the orca—is one of the top predators of the sea. The smallest—New Zealand's Hector's dolphin—is **endangered**. Some Asian river dolphins are **critically endangered**.

Why hands? It is the question Guido Daniele is asked most often. His answer may sound like a play on words. But they are important words, the words he lives by: "Because we must give animals a hand if they are to survive."

Hands are the most expressive part of the body after the face. We use them every day to do almost everything. Guido uses his own to transform hands into images of animals and plants. He hopes those images will help spread his belief that artists can convey a message with their art. "My message," he says, "is to protect nature, to protect life."

Body painting is one of the oldest forms of art, probably as old as cave or rock painting. It is still used in many cultures around the world. Guido's unique, clever designs were popular in fashion events and commercials when an ad agency asked him to paint animals on hands. It was a great idea! "People like to look at animals because they are the part of nature closest to us. They are beautiful. They have colors," he says. "I researched each animal to see how I could transfer it to a hand and bring it to life." The cheetah was his first hand painting.

Guido called his creations *Manimali*, or Handimals in English. Right away he realized he could use this art to spread his message of protecting and respecting nature. Handimals could help people understand the problem of animal extinction. Guido says, "I can always paint the image of a tiger, but it is impossible to create a living tiger once they are all gone."

Sometimes a Handimal starts with Guido himself. "I look at my hands and try to imagine all the different things they could turn into." Once he decides on a subject, he researches the animal and studies photographs for small details and distinct features. Planning and completing each Handimal takes a month or more.

Guido then goes on to choose the correct hand. Long, elegant hands are ideal, yet slightly square fingers might fit a project better. Unlike a canvas, skin has texture and is not flat. Guido takes advantage of natural wrinkles and lines, like those on the older model's hand he used for the Handimal elephant.

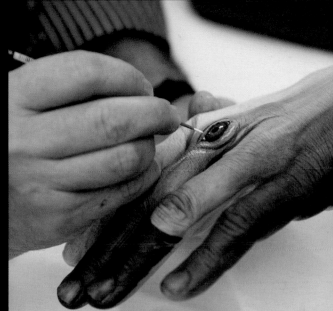

Next, the selected hand is photographed in different poses and without paint. Guido decides on the position that best fits the animal's shape. After making a detailed drawing on paper, the transformation—from human hand to Handimal—is ready to begin.

Guido starts by outlining the animal's features with special pencils. He takes great care when drawing the eyes. In an animal, the eye position, dimension, and expression are very important. He applies a base color all over the hand to make the skin tone even. Then, using different size brushes, he begins to paint the details—individual feathers, patterns of scales, fins, fur, and, of course, colors—that make this animal unique. Since regular art paints contain chemicals that could harm skin, Guido uses makeup. Not just any makeup, but natural powders mixed with water, like those used by actors in traditional Japanese theater.

It takes about three to four hours to paint and photograph a Handimal. Some require more than one model working together. Complicated images may take up to ten hours. The royal python, for example, used shoulders and elbows. And the mandarin duck required six

different hands! Painting and photography must be done in one day. Natural paints stay on for just a few hours. Plus, the models need their hands back! Guido uses computer programs to create backgrounds or combine images, like adding dozens of fingers to imitate grass. But he does not retouch the original paintings.

Guido works tirelessly for organizations like the World Wildlife Fund and Dolphin Aid. He has been named Animal Planet's Hero of the Year. One of his own heroes is Jane Goodall. He painted a chimpanzee Handimal on her hand to celebrate her eightieth birthday.

An interviewer once joked with Guido, calling him a man who is "all fingers and thumbs!" He has also been dubbed Michel*hand*gelo. "My art is very simple," he says. "I am happy to do something everybody understands, especially children."

SELECTED SOURCES

World Wildlife Fund: **worldwildlife.org** • International Union for Conservation of Nature: **iucn.org** • Defenders of Wildlife: **defenders.org**
National Geographic: **nationalgeographic.com/animals** • Smithsonian's National Zoo & Conservation Biology Institute: **nationalzoo.si.edu** • Additional resources at author's website: **silvialopezbooks.com**

TO MY CHILDREN: MARISA, ALINA, AND DANNY, MY OWN WORKS OF ART. —S.L.

*FOR JANE GOODALL AND THE "BLUE PLANET," OUR MOTHER, OUR HOME—THE ONLY PLACE
IN THE UNIVERSE WHERE PLANTS, ANIMALS, AND HUMANKIND CAN LIVE TOGETHER. —G.D.*

International management for Guido Daniele: aldoevents@gmx.de

*The author would like to thank Ron Magill,
communications director of Zoo Miami, for his expertise in reviewing this book.*

Photographs page 4 © CathyKeifer/Can Stock Photo Inc.; page 6 courtesy of iStock;
pages 8, 10, 24, 26, 32 courtesy of Wikimedia Commons;
page 12 by Petr Kratochvil, courtesy of Public Domain Pictures;
pages 14, 34 courtesy of Pexels; page 16 © Amwu/Dreamstime.com;
page 18 © Jerryway/Dreamstime.com; page 20 © Misscanon/Dreamstime.com;
page 22 © Katherineross4/Dreamstime.com; page 28 © Tamara Lee Harding/Dreamstime.com;
page 30 courtesy of Shutterstock.

Henry Holt and Company, *Publishers since 1866*
Henry Holt® is a registered trademark of Macmillan Publishing Group, LLC
175 Fifth Avenue, New York, NY 10010 • mackids.com

Library of Congress Cataloging-in-Publication Data
Names: Daniele, Guido, 1950– artist. | Lopez, Silvia, 1950– writer of added text.
Title: Handimals : animals in art and nature / Silvia Lopez ; art by Guido Daniele.
Description: New York : Henry Holt and Company, [2019] | "Christy Ottaviano books." |
 Audience: Ages 4–10.
Identifiers: LCCN 2018039231 | ISBN 9781627798914 (hardcover)
Subjects: LCSH: Animals in art—Juvenile literature. | Hand painting—Juvenile literature. |
Wildlife painting—Juvenile literature. | Animals—Miscellanea—Juvenile literature. |
Daniele, Guido, 1950- —Themes, motives.
Classification: LCC N7662 .D36 2019 | DDC 704.9/432—dc23
LC record available at https://lccn.loc.gov/2018039231

Our books may be purchased in bulk for promotional, educational, or business use.
Please contact your local bookseller or the Macmillan Corporate and Premium Sales Department
at (800) 221-7945 ext. 5442 or by email at MacmillanSpecialMarkets@macmillan.com.

First edition, 2019 / Designed by Erin Schell
Printed in China by Hung Hing Off-set Printing Co. Ltd., Heshan City, Guangdong Province

10 9 8 7 6 5 4 3 2 1